MR . LASTINGS The 1L

A Guide for the First Year Law Student

John Nemoy

Futilitarian Press

© 2012 John Nemoy

ISBN–13: 978–0615658483

ISBN–10: 0615658482

LIMIT OF LIABILITY

Disclaimer Of Warranty:

The cartoonist of this book (the "cartoonist") has used his reasonable efforts in preparing this book for your enjoyment; however, the cartoonist makes no representations or warranties with respect to the humor and/or the contents of this book and specifically disclaims any and all implied warranties of merchantability or fitness for a particular purpose. There are no warranties or representations, which extend beyond the description contained in this paragraph. No warranties or representations may be created or extended by the sales representatives of this book or any other person and/or entity. The cartoons (including without limitation the gags, jests, quips, witticisms, railleries, and/or japes) and the opinions stated in this book are not guaranteed or warranted to produce any particular result (e.g. laughing, chuckling, giggling, snickering, guffawing, tittering, cackling). The humor (or lack thereof) contained herein may not be suitable for every individual person (including without limitation, any firm partnership, corporation or entity). The cartoonist shall not be liable for any loss and/or any other commercial or noncommercial damages including but not limited to special, incidental, consequential or other damages now known or hereafter devised.

INTRODUCTION

Mr. Lastings* is your typical, average, semi-intelligent person. He has the same hopes and dreams as anyone. He fears the unknown. And to his dismay, he has just become a first year law student ("1L").

Why would he or anyone do this? There are many reasons: the pursuit of knowledge, to escape reality, to enjoy the prestigious life of an attorney, for the fun of it, or is it simply because everyone else is doing it? In any case, it doesn't really matter. Mr. Lastings wasn't the first, and he certainly won't be the last.

pronounced Lay-stings; rhymes with Hastings

For the 1L, the simple task of finding his or her seat is an ordeal. The 1L sheepishly staggers from one classroom to the next, only to find that the new class-room looks exactly like the old—same size, same dreary colors; even the students are the same. The only difference is the seating chart. It can be quite confusing.

Soon, after all 50+ intelligent people finally find their seats, the class begins. Here, the 1L may feel the shock and anguish of being randomly called upon by the professor. As all eyes seemingly fall upon the victim, he/she will struggle with the unwanted attention. The other 1L's will squirm in their seats and move as far from the victim as possible, thanking God that they were spared the professor's wrath.

This, of course, is the Socratic Method—active learning at its best. Here, the professor intersperses the boring lecture with poignant questions. However, there are no right answers to these questions. And, if by miracle a 1L finds the right answer, the 1L will receive another question and still another until the 1L gets one wrong and is berated by the professor. Is the 1L embarrassed? No! The 1L relishes in the fact that he/she will no longer be sought after.

CONGRATULATIONS FIRST YEAR LAW STUDENTS!
You are about to partake in a most interesting affair.

TO THOSE WHO ARE CURRENT MEMBERS OF THE BAR:
This book provides a chance to reminisce.

AND, TO THOSE NOT INVOLVED IN THE PROFESSION:
Sit back and enjoy! Learn how one becomes a lawyer and gain insight into why lawyers act the way they do. (And try to forget for a second that you hate lawyers.)

Mr. Lastings struggles. He struggles because we all struggle. However, his trials can be our chuckles and his tribulations our laughs.

ORIENTATION

LAW

Any system of regulations to govern the conduct
of the people of a community, society or nation, in
response to the need for regularity, consistency and
justice based upon collective human experience.

GREETINGS IN ENGLISH

GREETINGS IN LEGAL JARGON

LAWYER

An individual that is versed in the law. One who conducts lawsuits in the courts and advises clients of the law.

ATTORNEY

An individual who is appointed to act for another.

THE LIGHT AT THE END OF THE TUNNEL

AN ATTORNEY IN FACT
An individual who is appointed to act for another
in business or legal matters.

AN ATTORNEY AT LAW
A properly qualified legal agent who practices
in the courts.

ESQUIRE ("Esq.")
A title extended to men of the higher order of English gentry, or as a courtesy, extended to another person with an equivalent degree of rank or status.

A JOURNEY OF A THOUSAND MILES
BEGINS WITH A SINGLE STEP.

-Lao Tzu

WILDERNESS TIPS
FOR LAW STUDENTS

Accuracy and diligence are much more necessary to a lawyer than great comprehension of mind, or brilliancy of talent. His business is to refine, define, split hairs, look into authorities, and compare cases. A man can never gallop over the fields of law on Pegasus, nor fly across them on the wing of oratory. If he would stand on terra firma, he must descend. If he would be a great lawyer, he must first consent to become a great drudge.

–Daniel Webster

START BY DOING WHAT'S NECESSARY;
THEN DO WHAT'S POSSIBLE; AND
SUDDENLY YOU ARE DOING THE
IMPOSSIBLE.

-St. Francis of Assisi

THE LEARNING PROCESS BEGINS

FAILURE IS THE FOUNDATION
OF SUCCESS, AND THE MEANS
BY WHICH IT IS ACHIEVED.

-Lao Tzu

THE BEST WAY TO GET CALLED UPON

MY GREATEST CONCERN IS NOT
WHETHER YOU HAVE FAILED BUT
WHETHER YOU ARE CONTENT
WITH YOUR FAILURE.

-Abraham Lincoln

OUR GREATER GLORY IS NOT IN NEVER FAILING, BUT IN RISING EVERY TIME WE FALL.

-Confucius

LOOK BEFORE YOU LEAP;
SEE BEFORE YOU GO.

-Thomas Tusser

SECOND THOUGHTS

THINGS MAY COME TO THOSE
WHO WAIT, BUT ONLY THE THINGS
LEFT BY THOSE WHO HUSTLE.

-Abraham Lincoln

A BAD DAY   A REALLY BAD DAY

IF A MAN EMPTIES HIS PURSE INTO
HIS HEAD, NO MAN CAN TAKE IT
AWAY FROM HIM. AN INVESTMENT
IN KNOWLEDGE ALWAYS PAYS THE
BEST INTEREST.

- Benjamin Franklin

THERE IS NO MAN SO GOOD,
WHO, WERE HE TO SUBMIT ALL
HIS THOUGHTS AND ACTIONS TO
THE LAWS WOULD NOT DESERVE
HANGING TEN TIMES IN HIS LIFE.

-Michel Eyquem de Montaigne

A QUERY   A REPLY

Between two hawks, which flies the higher pitch;
Between two dogs, which hath the deeper mouth;
Between two blades, which bears the better temper;
Between two horses, which doth bear him best;
Between two girls; which hath the merriest eye,—
I have perhaps some shallow spirit of judgment;
But in these nice sharp quillets of the law,
Good faith, I am no wiser than a daw.

-*William Shakespeare*, **King Henry VI**

AND WHETHER YOU'RE AN HONEST
MAN OR WHETHER YOU'RE A THIEF
— DEPENDS ON WHOSE SOLICITOR
HAS GIVEN ME MY BRIEF.

-Benjamin Franklin

WHEN "UNDERSTANDING" HITS
THE FIRST YEAR STUDENT

LAWS CAN DISCOVER SIN,
BUT NOT REMOVE IT.

-John Milton

A QUERY   A REPLY

BUT WE KNOW THAT THE LAW IS GOOD, IF ONE USES IT LAWFULLY, REALIZING THE FACT THAT LAW IS NOT MADE FOR A RIGHTEOUS PERSON, BUT FOR THOSE WHO ARE LAWLESS AND REBELLIOUS, FOR THE UNGODLY AND SINNERS.

-1 Timothy 1 : 8–9 New Testament

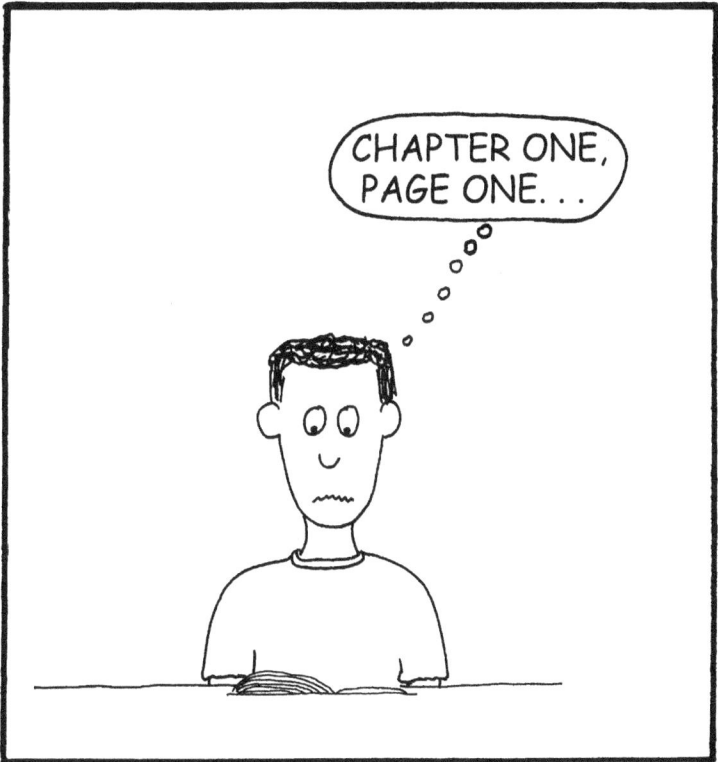

HAPPY THANKSGIVING

ONLY ONE THING IS IMPOSSIBLE
FOR GOD: TO FIND ANY SENSE
IN ANY COPYRIGHT LAW ON THE
PLANET.

-Mark Twain

WHICH STUDENT STUDIES TOO MUCH?

OUR DOUBTS ARE TRAITORS, AND MAKE US LOSE THE GOOD THAT WE OFT MAY WIN, BY FEARING TO ATTEMPT.

-William Shakespeare, **Measure for Measure**

IS IT NOT LAWFUL FOR ME TO DO
WHAT I WILL WITH MINE OWN?

-Matthew 20 : 15, **New Testament**

THE LEARNING PROCESS BEGINS... AGAIN

IF YOU MUST BREAK THE LAW, DO
IT TO SEIZE POWER: IN ALL OTHER
CASES OBSERVE IT.

-Julius Caesar

A WATCHED POT NEVER BOILS

A WATCHED CASE NEVER BRIEFS

SCIENCE FOR LAW STUDENTS

NECESSITY HAS NO LAW.

-Francois Rabelais

REASON IS THE LIFE OF THE LAW;
NAY, THE COMMON LAW ITSELF
IS NOTHING ELSE BUT REASON—
THE LAW, WHICH IS PERFECTION
OF REASON.

-Sir Edward Coke

DR. DOLITTLE GOES TO LAW SCHOOL

GOVERNMENT IS NOT MERE
ADVICE; IT IS AUTHORITY, WITH
POWER TO ENFORCE ITS LAWS.

-George Washington

WHAT PROFESSORS ASK AND . . . . . WHAT STUDENTS HEAR

QUICK! TURN OUT THE LIGHTS
BEFORE IT GETS DARK.

-John Nemoy

FIRST LOOK LEFT AND THEN RIGHT. ONE OF THEM
WON'T BE WITH YOU AT THE END OF THE YEAR.

GREAT WORKS ARE PERFORMED NOT
BY STRENGTH BUT BY PERSEVERANCE.

–Samuel Johnson

THE SOCRATIC METHOD

AT HIS BEST, MAN IS THE NOBLEST
OF ALL ANIMALS; SEPARATED
FROM LAW AND JUSTICE HE IS
THE WORST.

–Aristotle

THE FRESHMAN COMES
HOME FOR THE SUMMER

THE 1L COMES HOME
FOR THE SUMMER

LAW STANDS MUTE IN THE MIDST
OF ARMS.

–Marcus Tullius Cicero

WINTER BREAK

NEGLIGENCE IS THE RUST OF THE
SOUL THAT CORRODES THROUGH
ALL HER BEST RESOLVES.

-Owen Felltham

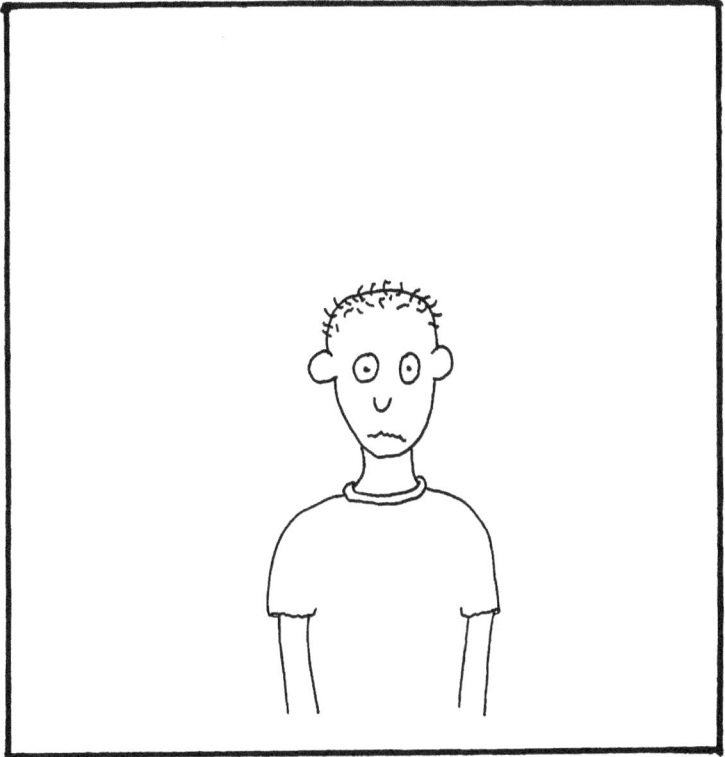

BLACK LETTER LAW: NEVER BE
SARCASTIC WITH YOUR BARBER

EVERY DUTY WHICH WE OMIT
OBSCURES SOME TRUTH WHICH
WE SHOULD HAVE KNOWN.

-John Ruskin

A LAWYER AFTER A GOOD DAY'S WORK

A MULTITUDE OF LAWS IN A COUNTRY IS LIKE A GREAT NUMBER OF PHYSICIANS, A SIGN OF WEAKNESS AND MALADY.

-François-Marie Arouet de Voltaire

ANOTHER YEAR WITH NOTHING TO DO

THE BEST WAY TO GET A BAD
LAW REPEALED IS TO ENFORCE
IT STRICTLY.

–Abraham Lincoln

NOBODY HAS A MORE SACRED
OBLIGATION TO OBEY THE LAW
THAN THOSE WHO MAKE THE LAW.

–Sophocles

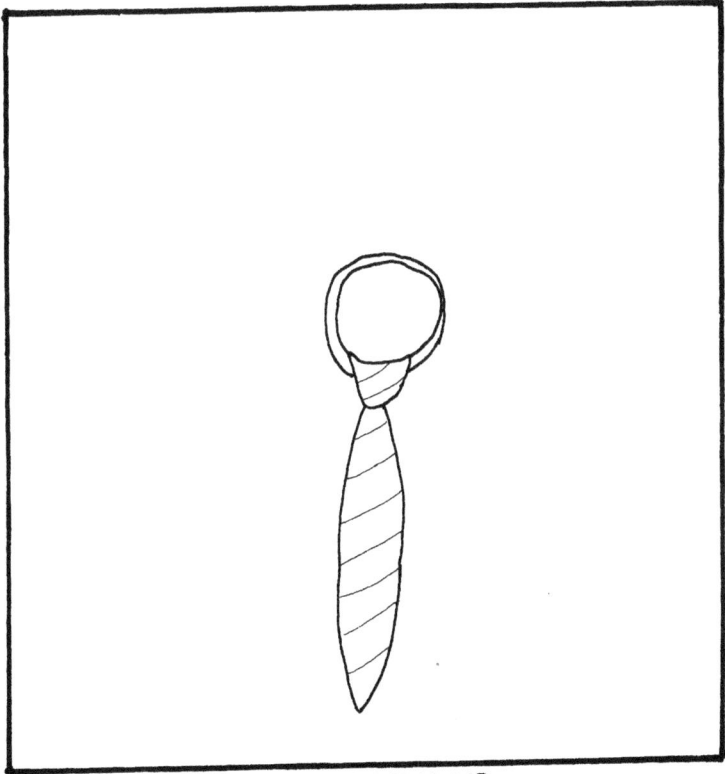

STRING HIM UP

LET US CONSIDER THE REASON OF THE
CASE. FOR NOTHING IS LAW THAT
IS NOT REASON.

-Sir John Powell

THE LAW IS THE LAST RESULT OF
HUMAN WISDOM ACTING UPON
HUMAN EXPERIENCE FOR THE
BENEFIT OF THE PUBLIC.

-*Samuel Johnson*

THE LAW IS A SORT OF HOCUS-POCUS SCIENCE THAT SMILES IN YER FACE WHILE IT PICKS YER POCKET: AND THE GLORIOUS UNCERTAINTY OF IT IS OF MORE USE TO THE PROFESSORS THAN THE JUSTICE OF IT.

–Charles Macklin

THINKING LIKE A LAWYER

A LAWYER WITHOUT HISTORY OR
LITERATURE IS A MECHANIC, A
MERE WORKING MASON; IF HE
POSSESSES SOME KNOWLEDGE
OF THESE, HE MAY VENTURE TO
CALL HIMSELF AN ARCHITECT.

-Sir Walter Scott

LAWS GRIND THE POOR, AND RICH
MEN RULE THE LAW.

-Oliver Goldsmith

JURISPRUDENCE IN AMERICA

THERE ARE ONLY 728,200 PEOPLE IN THE UNITED STATES EMPLOYED AS LAWYERS.

-2010 U.S. Department Of Labor, Bureau of Labor Statistics

INTELLECTUALS AT WORK

THE MEDIAN ANNUAL WAGE FOR A
LAWYER IN THE UNITED STATES IS
ONLY $112,760 PER YEAR.

-2010 U.S. Department Of Labor, **Bureau of Labor Statistics**

NO LAWS,

however stringent,

can make

the **idle** *industrious,*

the **thriftless** *provident,*

or the **drunken** *sober.*

–Samuel Smiles